COUNTDOWN TO SPACE

APOLLO II
First Moon Landing

Michael D. Cole

Series Advisor:
John E. McLeaish
Chief, Public Information Office, retired,
NASA Johnson Space Center

ENSLOW PUBLISHERS, INC.

44 Fadem Road   P.O. Box 38
Box 699   Aldershot
Springfield, N.J. 07081   Hants GU12 6BP
U.S.A.   U.K.

696205

Library of Congress Cataloging-in-Publication Data

Cole, Michael D.
    Apollo 11: first moon landing / Michael D. Cole.
        p. cm. — (Countdown to space)
    Includes bibliographical references and index.
    ISBN 0-89490-539-2
    1. Project Apollo (U.S.)—Juvenile literature. 2. Apollo 11 (Spacecraft)—Juvenile
literature. 3. Collins, Michael, 1930– —Juvenile literature. 4. Armstrong, Neil,
1930– —Juvenile literature. 5. Aldrin, Buzz—Juvenile literature. [1. Project Apollo
(U.S.) 2. Space flight to the moon.] I.Title. II. Series: Cole, Michael D. Countdown to
space.
TL789.8.U6A5265 1995
629.45′4— dc20   94-30001
                                                                           CIP
                                                                            AC

Printed in the U.S.A.

10 9 8 7 6 5 4 3 2 1

Illustration Credits:
National Aeronautics and Space Administration (NASA), pp. 4, 6, 7, 8, 9,
10, 11, 14, 16, 19, 23, 25, 26, 31, 32, 34, 35, 36, 37, 39, 40.

Cover Illustration:
National Aeronautics and Space Administration (NASA) (foreground);
© L. Manning/Westlight (background).

CONTENTS

Neil Armstrong, Michael Collins, and Buzz Aldrin will always be remembered for their heroic and historic flight aboard Apollo 11.

The Voyage Begins

It was warm on the morning of July 16, 1969, at Cape Kennedy in Florida. On launchpad 39A sat the mighty Saturn V rocket—the most powerful machine ever built. At the top of the towering rocket—363 feet above the ground—three men waited to begin mankind's most historic journey.

In the right couch was Michael Collins. He was the command module pilot. He would not land on the Moon, but he would orbit the Moon in the command module. The other two astronauts would make the landing on the Moon in the lunar module.

Collins was born in Rome, Italy, in 1930 while his father was stationed there with the U.S. Army. Collins had been an air force test pilot and had already been in space before. He flew in the *Gemini 10* mission, and he

had walked in space. He was married and had two daughters and a son. Collins liked to joke that because there was no TV set on the command module, he would be one of the few Americans who would not see the Moon landing.[1]

In the middle couch was Edwin E. Aldrin. He would co-pilot the lunar module, which was named *Eagle*. Everyone called him "Buzz." It had been his nickname since his childhood in Montclair, New Jersey. He was thirty-nine years old, and he also had been an air force pilot.

Aviation was in Aldrin's blood. His father had been a colonel in the U.S. Army Air Corps and was a friend of Orville Wright and

Awaiting liftoff, the Saturn V rocket sits on the launchpad.

Astronaut Michael Collins piloted the command module of Apollo 11.

Charles Lindbergh. His mother's maiden name was Marian Moon. Aldrin had been in space on *Gemini 12.* He held the record for the longest spacewalk. He was an intelligent and serious man who spoke in the precise manner of an engineer. He was married, with two sons and a daughter.

In the left couch was mission commander Neil A. Armstrong. He was from Wapakoneta, Ohio, where he had earned a pilot's license before he was old enough to drive a car. After flying as a Navy pilot he became an astronaut. He commanded the *Gemini 8* mission. Armstrong was probably the best pilot among all the astronauts. He was married and the father of two sons. His boyish smile made him look much younger than his thirty-eight years. Because he was mission commander, he would be the first person to walk upon the Moon.

These three men were about to experience an extraordinary adventure. All three had been in space before. All had been proud to serve their country in the space program. But they knew this mission was different.

People all over the world were waiting for the launch. They hoped *Apollo 11's* historic mission to land on the Moon would be a success. People everywhere felt that a part of themselves was going with those three astronauts. Armstrong, Aldrin, and Collins could not escape the fact that this time they did not just represent their country. This time they represented the human race.

The three astronauts suited up in their bulky spacesuits. Then they made the five-mile trip to the

launching pad in a large van. It went over a special remote route to avoid the incredible traffic jam that had been building around the Cape for days. Beaches and parks were full of camper trailers. Lakes and waterways were full of boats anchored where they could watch the launch. All

Edwin E. Aldrin, Jr., was nicknamed "Buzz." He was to be the second person ever to walk on the Moon.

Neil Armstrong will always be remembered as the first person to ever walk on the Moon. Armstrong was the mission commander of Apollo 11.

of them, and the nearly one billion people around the world who were watching the exciting countdown on television, waited to witness the historic moment when *Apollo 11* began its journey to the Moon.

"Two minutes and ten seconds and counting, and the Moon at this precise second is 218,986 miles away," the announcer said over the Cape loudspeaker.[2] The countdown was going smoothly. Armstrong, Aldrin, and Collins had trained for over a year for this mission. Now it was about to begin. Collins thought they had about a fifty-fifty chance of completing the mission successfully. Armstrong and Aldrin thought their chances were a little better. The three had never discussed the subject with each other.[3]

The countdown swept toward the final minute, then the final seconds. Armstrong wrapped his gloved hand around the abort handle in case the launch went badly. Aldrin looked at Armstrong and then turned to grin at Collins. They were finally going!

Collins remembered walking to the pad just a while ago. He had watched the frosty steam rolling off the rocket's sides when the warm air met the rocket filled with super-cooled liquid oxygen and hydrogen. He remembered thinking the rocket almost seemed *alive.*[4] Seconds from now, it would indeed rumble to life.

The loudspeaker at the Cape kept the thousands of onlookers counting toward the launch. "We are still go with *Apollo 11*. Thirty seconds and counting.

Armstrong, Collins, and Aldrin pose for a picture in front of the mighty Apollo/Saturn V rocket which would carry them to the Moon.

Astronauts reported, feel good . . . T minus twenty seconds and counting. T minus fifteen seconds, guidance is internal."

All power was now on in the *Apollo 11* spacecraft. Armstrong, Aldrin, and Collins were excited, but their minds were focused on the many tasks that had to be done.[5]

"Twelve, eleven, ten, nine, ignition sequence starts." Flame and smoke gushed from the five main engines of the Saturn V rocket. "Six, five, four, three, two, one, zero, all engines running." The controllers at the Cape pushed the engines to the proper thrust of 7.5 million pounds, equal to the power

At 9:32 A.M. on July 16, 1969, the three astronauts aboard the Apollo 11 *launched into their history-making flight.*

of more than 92,000 locomotives. Then they released the pad's hold-down clamps.

The mighty Saturn V, all 3,000 tons of it, rose from the launchpad.

"LIFT-OFF! We have a lift-off! Thirty-two minutes past the hour. Lift-off on Apollo 11." It was 9:32 A.M. The rocket's deafening rise through the sky could be seen and heard for miles around the Cape. The huge flaming thrust of the engines created a shock wave that could be *felt* for just as far. The powerful Saturn V climbed through the sky, pushing the three astronauts toward space while the whole world watched.

The exciting launch was a great success. Still, it was hard to believe what was about to happen. In four days, the men of *Apollo 11* would try to land on the Moon.

2

Bound for the Moon

Apollo 11 trailed a tongue of orange flame hundreds of feet long as it shot into space at incredible speed. After only two and a half minutes, the rocket was moving at nine thousand feet per *second.*

Control of the mission was switched from Cape Kennedy to the Manned Spacecraft Center (now called the Johnson Space Center) in Houston, Texas. "Thrust is go all engines. You're looking good," said Mission Control.[1]

"Roger," Armstrong said. The rapid acceleration pushed Armstrong, Aldrin, and Collins back into their couches. The large first stage of the Saturn V burned up its fuel and separated. Moments later the second stage cut in. It burned for about six minutes and boosted *Apollo 11* to 114 miles above the Earth. As they reached a speed of 15,000 miles per hour, the second stage also separated.

The single engine on the third stage then ignited. It burned for about two minutes. "Shutdown," Armstrong reported, as the engine shut down right on schedule. The three astronauts now felt themselves floating against their straps. They were in orbit around the Earth.

Armstrong, Aldrin, and Collins looked out their windows to see the beautiful Earth below. Their bubblelike helmets let them turn and see in any direction. The headgear covering their heads and ears looked like an old pilot's cap. It included earphones and two microphones for the astronauts to communicate with Mission Control. The white space suits they wore were made specially to fit each one of them. Each suit cost up to one million dollars.

Switches, buttons, dials, and readouts surrounded them on all sides of their

Apollo 11's *powerful rocket booster generated 7.5 million pounds of thrust to send the spacecraft on its journey to the Moon.*

positions in the command module (named *Columbia*). All the instruments had to be checked before they fired the third stage engine again to leave Earth's orbit. They removed their helmets and gloves and went to work. Collins folded down the bottom half of his couch and moved into the lower equipment bay. He made navigational sightings and passed out cameras and other equipment to Armstrong and Aldrin. About three hours later they were ready for the next phase of their journey.

"*Apollo 11,* this is Houston. You are Go for TLI."

TLI meant Translunar Injection. The third-stage rocket engine ignited again and burned for more than six minutes. When it cut off, they were travelling at 24,300 miles per hour. *Apollo 11* had left Earth's gravity and was on its way to the Moon.

"Hey, Houston, that Saturn gave us a magnificent ride," Armstrong told Mission Control.

Now Collins had to show his stuff. He pushed a button and freed the command module (CM) from the Saturn rocket. With his left hand he pushed a control handle forward; this moved the CM ahead of the rocket. Then he turned the CM around to face the rocket. The rocket housed the lunar module (LM) directly behind where the CM had been. Carefully, he moved the CM back to the rocket to dock with the LM. Once they were docked nose-to-nose, he threw a switch and the LM sprang free of the spent third-stage rocket.

The astronauts were able to see the beauty of Earth from space. This photo taken from Apollo 11 *shows parts of Africa, Europe, and Asia.*

Collins turned the CM back around and gave its engine a two-second burst. The CM, named *Columbia,* and the LM, named *Eagle,* were now set for their three-day trip to the Moon.

Armstrong, Collins, and Aldrin helped each other take off their bulky spacesuits. They felt much more comfortable in their two-piece white nylon jumpsuits. Armstrong looked out his window at Earth. He described for Mission Control what he saw of the North and South American continents. Ten hours after the launch, the astronauts did a short TV broadcast from *Columbia*. They pointed the camera back at Earth for a while. Then they showed the TV viewers around the inside of the two spacecrafts. This and other broadcasts were a big hit.

The astronauts then got a chance to sleep. Collins slept with a tiny headset taped to his ear in case Mission Control had an urgent message. When they awoke several hours later, the view of Earth barely filled one window.

The astronauts spent the next three days keeping the spacecrafts in good working order. They had to charge batteries, dump waste water, purge fuel cells, prepare food, purify drinking water, and make a mid-course correction.

Whenever Mission Control woke the astronauts from their sleep, the capcom (capsule communicator) would give them a brief update on news from Earth. Much of that news concerned stories about their flight. One of the reports was about President Richard Nixon.

"President Nixon has declared a day of participation on Monday for all federal employees," the capcom said, "to enable everybody to follow your activities on the surface." The astronauts were scheduled to land on the Moon late Sunday and make their Moonwalk early Monday. "It looks like you're going to have a pretty big audience."

On Friday, the third day of the mission, *Apollo 11* was 214,000 miles from Earth. At this point the Moon's gravity had a stronger influence on the spacecraft than Earth's gravity. They only had 38,000 miles to go until they entered lunar orbit. The image of the Moon began to grow steadily outside their windows.

During one of their TV broadcasts, Collins was shown alone at *Columbia's* controls. "Is Collins going to go in the lunar module and look around?" asked Mission Control.

"We'd like to let him," Armstrong said jokingly, "but he hasn't come up with the price of a ticket." Collins always insisted that he did not feel badly that he was the one staying behind while Armstrong and Aldrin made the Moon landing. He was happy just to be in space again. Collins had missed an earlier space mission because of surgeries to remove a bone spur that was pressing on nerves along his upper spine. He felt fortunate to have recovered. He was very excited to be assigned to the historic first Moon-landing mission. It would be his last spaceflight.[2]

Buzz Aldrin was a little disappointed that he would not be the first to set foot on the Moon. It was NASA's decision that Armstrong would go down the ladder first. But Armstrong and Aldrin would be making the landing together. They would be the first people on the Moon. That alone was quite an honor. Aldrin also knew that Armstrong was a superb pilot. He wouldn't have wanted to make the difficult landing with anyone else.[3]

Many people had asked Armstrong what he was going to say when he first stepped on the Moon. He had never really had the spare time to think about that. He had been too busy with training and meetings and studying for the mission. As they neared the Moon now, he began to think about it a little. He decided he would never really know what to say until he and Aldrin had actually landed on the Moon.[4]

The Moon as viewed from Apollo 11.

By Day Four of the mission the Moon's appearance had changed dramatically in the astronauts' eyes. Armstrong, Aldrin, and Collins saw the Moon as a three-dimensional thing for the first time. It was the most awesome sphere they had ever seen. It completely filled their window. Armstrong tried to describe what they were seeing.

"The view of the Moon . . . is really spectacular," he said. "We can see the entire circumference even though part of it is in complete shadow and part of it is in Earthshine (sunlight reflected off the Earth). It's a view worth the price of the trip."

"We're able to see stars again and recognize constellations for the first time on the trip," Collins added. "The Earthshine coming through the window is so bright you can read a book by it."

They could not linger by the windows for long. They were about to pass behind the dark side of the Moon. They would lose contact with Earth for more than thirty minutes. During that time they would fire *Columbia*'s engines to slow themselves down and get into lunar orbit. If it worked, their next step would be to prepare *Eagle* for its descent to the Moon.

3

The Landing

Apollo *11* swung around the dark side of the Moon, losing radio contact with Mission Control. During this first radio blackout the three astronauts and their spacecraft were now in orbit around the Moon.

Coming around on their first orbit, Apollo *11* regained radio contact. The astronauts got their first view of some important sights on the Moon's surface. "We're getting our first view of the landing site approach," Armstrong said. "The pictures brought back by Apollos *8* and *10* have given us a pretty good preview of what to look at here. It looks very much like the pictures, but . . . there's no substitute for actually being here."[1]

So far the mission was going incredibly well. Armstrong, Aldrin, and Collins settled down to rest before the big day tomorrow. They slept only five or six hours, the shortest rest period of the flight. When they awoke on Sunday, it was time to do what they had been practicing to do for over a year. But this time it would be for real.

Aldrin crawled down the tunnel and through the hatch into *Eagle*. He powered up the spacecraft and ran through a series of systems checks. Armstrong joined him a short time later. The checks continued and everything was go.

"*Apollo,* Houston. We're go for undocking," reported Mission Control. The radio again blacked out, and they swung around the Moon's dark side on their thirteenth orbit. Armstrong and Aldrin extended the landing legs on *Eagle*. After nearly ten years of hard work, the goal of the manned space program was about to be realized. They were ready to go for the landing.

Collins pressed a button in the command module. Latches clicked open, and *Eagle* floated gently away from *Columbia*. Mission Control waited for the signal to come through again. As *Eagle* again came into radio contact, Armstrong announced through the static, "The *Eagle* has wings."

The two ships flew in formation while Collins inspected the lunar module for any problems or damage. "Looks like you've got a mighty good-looking flying machine there, *Eagle*," he said, "despite the fact that you're upside down." Collins later gave *Columbia* a burst from its engine. This boosted him ahead to give *Eagle* some flying room. "OK *Eagle* . . . you guys take care."

"See you later," Armstrong said.

Eagle was again on the dark side, in radio blackout. It began its long arcing descent toward the landing site. The site was in an area on the Moon called the Sea of Tranquility. This place was chosen as a landing site because the area was wide-open and very flat. If all went well, Armstrong and Aldrin would land there in about seventeen minutes. They came out of the radio

"The Eagle *has wings"* announced Armstrong as the lunar module separated from the command module.

blackout with everything going fine. *Eagle* had now descended to about ten miles above the lunar surface.

"You are go to continue powered descent," Mission Control said. "You're looking good."

"Got the Earth right out our front window," Aldrin said. Armstrong had turned *Eagle* into position; its landing legs were pointed toward the lunar surface. This enabled the landing radar to lock on and feed altitude and velocity data to the onboard computer. The landing proceeded perfectly as Armstrong and Aldrin descended to 3,000 and then 2,000 feet from the surface. Then things got very tense. An alarm light flashed on their instrument panels.

"Twelve alarm," Aldrin said, "1201." This meant that one of the landing computers was overloaded with data. It was feeding Armstrong and Aldrin faulty information about their descent.

"Roger," said Mission Control, "1201 alarm." The controllers at Houston assured them the computer would reset. They were to continue the descent despite the alarm.

"We're go," Aldrin replied. "Hang tight. We're go. Two thousand feet." Aldrin continued to read out the data. Armstrong watched out his left window as they approached the landing site. "Seven hundred feet, 21 down," Aldrin said. This meant *Eagle* was seven hundred feet above the Moon and was descending at twenty-one feet per second. "Four hundred feet, down

The controllers at Mission Control in Houston were anxiously awaiting the lunar landing.

at 9. We're pegged on horizontal velocity. Three hundred feet, down 3 and a half."

The controllers in Houston were on the edge of their seats. Nearly every astronaut in the astronaut program was gathered behind the viewing window in the control room. They were all nervously watching the television screen and listening to Aldrin call out the landing data.[2]

"Altitude-velocity lights. Three and a half down, 220 feet. Thirteen forward, 11 forward, coming down nicely. Two hundred feet, 4 and a half down, 5 and half down."

The landing site came into view outside *Eagle's* two

windows. As Armstrong looked, he saw something that made his heartbeat begin to race.[3] The computer was leading *Eagle* to the intended landing site. But that site was littered with boulders the size of automobiles! There was no way they could make a safe landing among those boulders.

Armstrong grasped the rocket control handle with his right hand and overrode the automatic landing system. *Eagle* skimmed over the large field of boulders as Armstrong searched the lunar surface for a smoother landing area. He knew he had to find it in a hurry. *Eagle* was now only one hundred feet above the Moon, and

View of the approaching landing site on the Moon, as seen by the astronauts aboard Apollo 11.

its landing engine was running very close to the end of its fuel.

"Seventy five feet," Aldrin continued. "Down a half, 6 forward."

"Sixty seconds," Mission Control said, meaning there was only one minute of fuel left in *Eagle's* landing engine. The controllers in Houston were unaware of the boulders Armstrong had seen. They were anxious for Armstrong to set *Eagle* down.[4]

"Forty feet, down 2 and a half," Aldrin read out to Armstrong, who was flying *Eagle* toward a spot he saw several hundred yards to the right of his window. Getting there would be cutting it very close. "Picking up some dust. Thirty feet . . . faint shadow. Four forward, drifting to the right a little."

"Thirty seconds," said Mission Control.

"Six forward. Drifting right." *Eagle* was now kicking up a lot of dust on the surface. "Contact light." This meant that one of the feelers on the legs of the lunar module had touched the Moon. The cloud of dust moved away from them. Armstrong and Aldrin sensed that they and *Eagle* had come to a complete stop. They were motionless.

Almost out of habit, Aldrin continued to read out the information from his panel. "Okay, engine stop. . . . descent engine command override, off. Engine arm, off."

All of Mission Control's instruments told the

controllers that the lunar module was down. "We copy you down, *Eagle,*" came the communicator's voice.

"Houston," Armstrong replied, hesitating for a moment, "Tranquility Base here. The Eagle has landed."

Mission Control erupted in cheers. "Roger Tranquility," the communicator said through the noise, "we copy you on the ground. You've got a bunch of guys about to turn blue. We're breathing again. Thanks a lot."

Aldrin reached across his instrument panel and he and Armstrong shook hands firmly. They had done it! Looking out their windows, they stared with awe at the stark and lonely alien landscape.[5] It was hard to believe they were really on the Moon.

A quarter of a million miles away, people all over the Earth were slowly realizing what had just happened. Human beings had for the first time landed upon another world.

4

One Giant Leap

Mission Control was still loud with the excitement of the landing. "Be advised there are lots of smiling faces in this room and all over the world. Over," the communicator told the astronauts.[1]

"There are two of them up here," Armstrong replied.

"And don't forget one in the command module," Collins broke in on the circuit. "Tranquility Base, it sure sounded good from here. You guys did a fantastic job."

"Thank you," Armstrong replied. "Just keep that orbiting base ready for us up there now."

Armstrong and Aldrin were scheduled for a four-hour rest period after the landing systems check. They were simply too excited. They requested to go ahead with preparations for the Moon walks now.[2] Houston agreed. The two astronauts ate their first meal on the Moon. Then they spent the next two hours getting suited up for the Moon walks.

The suits Armstrong and Aldrin wore included a backpack that would keep a person alive on the Moon for four hours. It carried oxygen for them to breathe, water to cool the special garment they wore beneath the suit, and communications equipment. As soon as Armstrong and Aldrin sealed their helmets and gloves, they depressurized the cabin. Armstrong dropped to his hands and knees and began to back out of the open hatch. He stepped onto the ladder on one of *Eagle's* landing legs.

Back on Earth, millions breathlessly watched their televisions. A camera placed near the base of the lunar module brought them live pictures of Armstrong's ghostly image coming down the ladder. People all over the world were amazed that astronauts were on the Moon. And most of them found it just as amazing that they were able to watch live television pictures of it.

"Okay Neil, we can see you coming down the ladder now," Mission Control said.

Armstrong carefully stepped down each rung of the ladder. It was tricky. He was still getting used to the bulky suit and the Moon's gravity, which is one-sixth the gravity of Earth. "I'm at the foot of the ladder," Armstrong reported. "The LM footpads are only

Stepping down from the lunar module to the Moon was tricky. Above is Buzz Aldrin descending the ladder.

depressed in the surface about one or two inches. Although the surface appears to be very, very fine grained, as you get close to it. It's almost like a powder."

The Mission Control room was completely silent. They were fascinated by every word of Armstrong's description of the Moon's landscape around him. They knew they were witnessing history.

"I'm going to step off the LM now." Armstrong

moved his left leg away from *Eagle's* footpad and planted his boot in the lunar soil—the first human step on another world. "That's one small step for a man . . . one giant leap for mankind."

Millions of people on Earth witnessed this moment of history. It was a moment unlike any other. It gave many people a sense of awe and a feeling of pride that humanity had accomplished such a feat. It left many people, including the famous CBS television news anchor Walter Cronkite, completely speechless.

Armstrong walked around the landing area. His walk looked more like a bouncy skip or a hop. The Moon's gravity allowed him to bound lightly from one foot to the other. He took out a scoop with a long handle to collect the first sample of Moon soil. He collected some soil and rocks in a bag and placed it in a pocket just above his left knee. Then he looked out across the lunar landscape.

Neil Armstrong's bootprints in the lunar soil mark the spot where he made the famous statement, "That's one small step for a man . . . one giant leap for mankind."

"It has a stark beauty all its own," he said. "It's different, but it's very pretty out here."

A few minutes later, Aldrin joined Armstrong on the surface. "Beautiful view!" Aldrin said when he stepped away from the ladder.

"Isn't that something?" Armstrong said. "Magnificent sight out here."

"Magnificent desolation," Aldrin added.

They practiced different methods of walking in Moon's gravity and reported their sensations to Mission Control. Then they unveiled a plaque attached to *Eagle*'s landing leg. Armstrong read it for the viewers back on Earth.

"'Here Men from the planet Earth first set foot upon the Moon, July 1969 AD. We came in peace for all mankind.' It has the crewmembers' signatures and the signature of the President of the United States."

Next they planted the United States flag near *Eagle* and received a special telephone call from President Richard Nixon.

"For one priceless moment, in the whole history of man," Nixon said, "all the people of Earth are truly one. One in their pride in what you have done. And one in our prayers that you will return safely to Earth."

The two astronauts went to work setting up a number of scientific experiments. They assembled a laser ranging retro-reflector that would measure the exact distance between the Earth and the Moon for the

Aldrin poses near the special American flag which the astronauts put on the Moon. Since there is no wind on the Moon, the flag was stiffened to look as if it was blowing. The lunar module is seen on the left.

first time. A seismic detector was set up to measure shock vibrations or "Moonquakes" on the lunar surface. It was so sensitive that when it was working, the scientists on Earth could detect the astronauts footsteps.

A foil-like solar wind flag was unfurled to collect particles, gases, and other elements that reached the Moon from the sun. It would later be rolled up and stowed aboard *Eagle* for the trip back to Earth.

Armstrong and Aldrin collected many containers of lunar soil and rocks. Scientists hoped they would learn much about the Moon and its origin, and perhaps the origin of the Earth, from this lunar soil. This was the primary scientific purpose of sending astronauts to the Moon.

Armstrong and Aldrin spent about three hours on their Moon walk. Then they stowed all the soil samples and equipment inside *Eagle* and closed the hatch behind them. It was a long process to climb out of their bulky, and now very dirty, suits. They ate another meal, then tried to get some sleep in the seatless and now very cramped cabin of *Eagle.*

When they awoke it was time to prepare for *Eagle's* launch from the Moon. About twenty-one and a half

Aldrin sets up the foil-like solar wind flag to collect samples of lunar air particles.

The lunar module as viewed by Collins aboard the command module on its ascent from the Moon.

hours after *Eagle* had landed on the Moon, it was ready to take off again.

The countdown ticked to zero and the ascent engine fired perfectly. The upper part of *Eagle* launched Armstrong and Aldrin and their cargo of lunar soil away from the Moon. They left the descent engine and landing legs behind on the surface.

Six hours later they docked with *Columbia*. Collins grabbed Aldrin's head with both hands and almost kissed him as he floated through the hatch. The three of them loaded the soil samples and equipment into *Columbia* and resealed the hatch. Collins flipped a switch that released some clamps. *Eagle* was cast away to eventually crash on the Moon. Armstrong and Aldrin were sad to see it go.[3] It had served them well.

The three astronauts prepared to fire *Columbia*'s engine once more. This "burn" would free them from the Moon's gravity and send them back toward Earth. As they swung around to the light side of the Moon, they saw the Earth rise over the lunar horizon. The engine burned for two and a half minutes, and Armstrong told Houston it was a success.

"Roger," said Mission Control. "We got you coming home."

As the astronauts began their trip home, they saw a spectacular view of the Earth rising over the moonscape.

5

Return to Earth

Two and a half days later, on Thursday, July 24, 1969, *Apollo 11* reentered the Earth's atmosphere. After the fiery reentry, huge red and white parachutes sprang from the nose of the capsule. Neil Armstrong, Edwin E. "Buzz" Aldrin, and Mike Collins came to a soft splashdown in the Pacific Ocean. *Apollo 11* had returned.

They were recovered by the aircraft carrier U.S.S. *Hornet.* President Nixon was waiting to welcome them. Scientists were afraid that the astronauts might have brought dangerous organisms back from the Moon. So the men had to wear strange airtight overalls with headgear that looked like gas masks.

As soon as a helicopter landed them on the carrier, they entered a large van that looked like a camper trailer. It was a comfortable quarantine facility. They took off the suits and looked out a window to participate in a welcoming ceremony with President Nixon. They stayed in the trailerlike facility for three days. Then it was flown by cargo plane to Houston. There it was pulled into the Lunar Receiving Laboratory (LRL). There the astronauts were let out of the trailer and scientists checked them out thoroughly.

For the next three weeks, Armstrong, Aldrin, and Collins lived in the LRL. They debriefed NASA people about the flight and were continually examined for the effects of any possible alien organisms. After three weeks, on August 10, 1969, the quarantine was over. The astronauts were released to the outside world.

President Richard M. Nixon proudly greets the three astronauts who were being quarantined aboard the U.S.S. Hornet.

The city of Chicago welcomes Armstrong, Collins, and Aldrin home with a tickertape parade.

For the next two months, Neil Armstrong, Buzz Aldrin, and Mike Collins rode in parades and gave speeches to hundreds of thousands of people on a tour that took them to six continents. They were heroes, and now an important part of history. Eventually the celebrations died down and plans for the next trip to the Moon, *Apollo 12*, continued. But there would never be another Moon mission like *Apollo 11*.

It is difficult to know the true meaning or importance of humanity's first voyage to another world. Perhaps Buzz Aldrin stated it best in his words to a joint session of Congress, fifty-four days after *Apollo 11* had returned from the Moon:

> *I say to you today what no men have been privileged to say before: We walked on the Moon. But the footprints at Tranquility Base belong to more than the crew of* Apollo 11. . . . *Those footprints belong to the American people . . . who accepted and supported the inevitable challenge of the Moon. And, since we came in peace for all mankind, those footprints belong also to all the people of the world.*
>
> *The first step on the Moon was a step toward our sister planets and ultimately the stars. 'A small step for a man' was a statement of fact, 'a giant leap for mankind' is a hope for the future.*[1]

CHAPTER NOTES

Chapter 1

1. John Barbour, *Footprints on the Moon* (New York: The Associated Press, 1969), p. 184.

2. *Apollo 11, Technical Air-to-Ground Voice Transcription,* Manned Spacecraft Center, Houston, Texas, July 1969. All in-flight communications which follow come from this source.

3. "Spaceflight Part 3: One Giant Leap," narrated by Martin Sheen, PBS Video (1985).

4. Michael Collins, *Carrying the Fire: An Astronaut's Journey* (New York: Farrar, Straus & Giroux, 1974), p. 418.

5. Ibid., p. 419.

Chapter 2

1. *Apollo 11, Technical Air-to-Ground Voice Transcription,* Manned Spacecraft Center, Houston, Texas, July 1969. All in-flight communications which follow come from this source.

2. Peter Bond, *Heroes in Space: From Gagarin to Challenger* (New York: Basil Blackwell, Inc., 1987), pp. 185–186.

3. Douglas MacKinnon and Joseph Baldanza, *Footprints* (Washington, D.C.: Acropolis Books Ltd., 1989), pp. 34–36.

4. Ibid., p. 288.

Chapter 3

1. *Apollo 11, Technical Air-to-Ground Voice Transcription,* Manned Spacecraft Center, Houston, Texas, July 1969. All in-flight communications which follow come from this source.

2. John Barbour, *Footprints On The Moon* (New York: The Associated Press, 1969), p. 205.

3. Peter Bond, *Heroes in Space: From Gagarin to Challenger* (New York: Basil Blackwell, Inc., 1987), p. 191.

4. Barbour, p. 206.

5. Harry Hurt III, *For All Mankind* (New York: Atlantic Monthly Press, 1988), p. 169.

Chapter 4

1. *Apollo 11, Technical Air-to-Ground Voice Transcription,* Manned Spacecraft Center, Houston, Texas, July 1969. All in-flight communications which follow come from this source.

2. Edwin E. "Buzz" Aldrin, Jr., with Wayne Warga, *Return to Earth* (New York: Random House, 1973), pp. 232–233.

3. Michael Collins, *Liftoff!* (New York: Grove Press, 1988), p. 31.

Chapter 5

1. Douglas MacKinnon and Joseph Baldanza, *Footprints* (Washington, D.C.: Acropolis Books Ltd., 1989), p. 21.

GLOSSARY

altitude—The distance of an airplane, spacecraft, or any other object from the ground or sea level.

automatic landing system—The system aboard the Apollo lunar module that used sensors and computers to guide the spacecraft to a predetermined landing site.

capcom (capsule communicator)—The person at Mission Control, usually another astronaut, who communicates directly with the astronauts in the spacecraft.

command module—The Apollo spacecraft that carried three astronauts into orbit around the Moon. It also carried the astronauts back home for reentry into Earth's atmosphere.

depressurize—Allowing the Earthlike atmosphere inside a spacecraft to escape out an opened hatch. This happens whenever an astronaut prepares to go outside the ship in a spacesuit. The suit provides the astronaut with the needed pressurized atmosphere.

Earthshine—The shine in space created by sunlight reflecting off the Earth's atmosphere and surface.

laser ranging retro-reflector—An instrument placed on the Moon by *Apollo 11* to measure the exact distance of the Moon from Earth.

lunar module—The Apollo spacecraft that landed two astronauts on the Moon and brought them back up to meet with the command module.

Lunar Receiving Laboratory—Facility where astronauts stayed while scientists checked the *Apollo 11* astronauts for three weeks following their flight.

quarantine facility—A facility used to isolate people from others, in order to prevent the spread of dangerous organisms or contagious disease.

Sea of Tranquility—A flat, open area on the surface of the Moon. It was chosen as the safest landing site for the first Moon landing mission because of its flatness.

seismic detector—A device used to detect and measure ground tremors or earthquakes. This device was used on the Moon to measure "Moonquakes."

solar wind flag—This device was set up on the Moon during *Apollo 11*. It was made of a special material that "caught" particles that had traveled to the Moon from the sun. The material was rolled up and brought back to Earth, so that scientists could study the sun particles it had collected.

translunar injection (TLI)—The name for when a spacecraft breaks out of Earth orbit and is put on a course toward the Moon. This process requires the spacecraft to reach a speed of more than 24,000 miles per hour.

velocity—The rate of speed of an object in a given direction.

FURTHER READING

Aldrin, Buzz, and Malcolm McConnell. *Men From Earth: An Apollo Astronaut's Exciting Account of America's Space Program*. New York: Bantam Books, 1989.

Barbour, John. *Footprints on the Moon*. New York: The Associated Press, 1969.

Bond, Peter. *Heroes in Space: From Gagarin to Challenger*. New York: Basil Blackwell, Inc., 1987.

Collins, Michael. *Carrying the Fire: An Astronaut's Journey*. New York: Farrar, Straus & Giroux, 1974.

Collins, Michael. *Liftoff!* New York: Grove Press, 1988.

Hurt, Harry III. *For All Mankind*. New York: Atlantic Monthly Press, 1988.

Gold, Susan. *Countdown to the Moon*. New York: Crestwood House, 1992.

Kennedy, Gregory P. *Apollo to the Moon*. New York: Chelsea House, 1992.

INDEX